Java Prog
Beginners

That guidebook for absolute beginners with no programming knowledge whatsoever

Introduction

Java is one of the most popular programming languages today. For one thing it is the programming language preferred by pretty much everyone when it comes to Android programming. Want to know how to develop apps for your smartphone? Learn how to program in this language!

Java is widely employed for the development of secure and robust web applications, mobile apps, enterprise applications, and desktop apps as well.

This book is geared towards people who have absolutely no idea about programming. You will learn programming concepts and nuances starting from the very fundamentals while you pick up on the details of Java Programming.

Now, isn't Java kind of complicated?

Now, that is an interesting question. Well, doesn't every kind of programming look complex from the start? The same thing is true with Java. Things will clear up rather quickly as soon as you understand the basics which will be your building blocks for the later stuff that you will include in the apps and programs that you will build.

Java actually presents you with a few benefits that outmatch other programming languages today.

1. It is the one programming language that is most commonly used today.

In other words it is the de facto standard. In today's extremely connected world, Java is the language code that operates and resided in more than 3 billion devices—this is according to Oracle.

Java is also consistently the most popular programming language from month to month, which is according to the

TIOBE Programming Community Index. And why is it a consistent favorite among many programmers today?

One of the reasons cited for its popularity is its plethora of real world applications. On top of that, since it is very popular you will find a lot of FREE support from a worldwide Java programming community. In case you get stuck while writing your code, you can find lots of help online.

2. It is a very good precursor for those who want to learn how to code.

Some people might recommend C, C#, or some other programming language to help absolute beginners learn how to write code. But guess what. Java is on the same level. In fact, in certain phases of the programming process, Java outperforms other programming languages.

Java is a core programming language—it's different from JavaScript (we'll get to that later). You can program your Java code for web as well as non-web environments. It is a programming language that works on all operating systems. On top of that it is also a programming language that works on all types of devices.

3. It makes you think like a programmer.

The nuances of Java programming will make you see and think things through like a professional programmer. Sure you will learn the different concepts and constructs of this programming language but along the way you will also learn the underpinnings of writing code.

Apart from that, you will also learn object orient programming (or OOP for short). To really master OOP you will be required to go up a notch from the good old top down design programming. Through Java you will learn to see things in both abstract and specific design which will give you a good base in this level of programming logic.

4. Java is an all-time pro.

Java has been around for more than 2 decades. Now, you might ask, how in the world is that going to help. Well, that means every problem you encounter or question that comes up to your mind already has an answer. There are no surprises whatsoever that someone out there hasn't fixed yet.

Apart from that, learning Java programming will open the way for you to create openings in many developer jobs that are definitely well-paying. This is a great language for beginners to start learning how to code.

We'll go over all of that and beyond as we go over the basics of Java programming for absolute beginners.

Thank you again for downloading this book.

Chapter 1: Introduction to Java and a Tiny Bit of Geekiness

Java is both a programming language that you can use for application development. It is a programming language that you can use to create and develop programs and applications. It is in fact one of most commonly used programming languages today.

This programming language was developed by Sun Microsystems back in 1995. The company was later acquired by Oracle. Note that Java is more than just a programming language – it is a complete platform.

What is a Programming Language?

A *computer program* is a set of instructions that a computer will perform. *Running* a program or *executing* a program means that a computer is carrying out the instructions that you have written in a computer program.

A programming language is like any other language that we speak (e.g. English, French, Greek, Japanese etc.). The difference is that a *programming language* is designed and structured so that you can construct a computer program. Programming languages have their own equivalent of grammar, vocabulary, and other rules.

There are several types of computer programming languages. Some are called high level languages and some are called low level languages. A high level programming language is one that resembles human speech. A low level programming language on the other hand is one that is more like the electronic signals that computers use.

Java is a high level programming language. Other programming languages that fall in the same category include C, C#, C++, Pascal, Javascript (yes, it's different from Java), and BASIC among others. These language resemble human speech and you may even be able to figure out what some parts of the program code does by just reading them line by line.

The Java Programming Platform

Don't be afraid of the term "platform." It's just a fancy way of saying that the makers of the Java programming language have created the complete package so that you can write programming code using their language.

The Java platform (i.e. the programming package) contains a lot of other apps and programs to assist you when you write your computer code. The package contents include the following:

- ***An execution engine*** – this is a program that executes or runs the code that you wrote so you can see it in action.
- ***A compiler*** – this is a program or app that translates the computer code that you wrote into a language that a computer can understand (we'll go over this later).
- ***A set of Java libraries*** – this isn't a physical library but it is a library of sorts. Think of it as a collection of books (it's actually a collection of different smaller programs that you can add to your programming code). The books are organized into sections and each section can be used to control different functions of a computer (or

phone or whatever device you want to program). Examples of these functions include how images and texts are displayed on screen, how a device or computer user can enter data or information, how the data will be used to create an output that the user can use.

What's interesting about Java (and this is one of its many advantages) is that it is an independent language. It doesn't matter whether you are creating a program for a phone running iOS, a computer that is run on Windows, or a car running its own proprietary software. Java works on all of these platforms (aka operating systems).

Beginner Programming Concepts – Basic Parts of Your Computer

To understand how programming languages like Java work we need to understand some of the basics of computer technology. A computer is any device that is capable of making computations and performing actions at super-fast speeds.

That means the term "computer" can technically refer to not just the huge desktop computers or even the laptops we use in our offices and homes. It can include our phones, our TV, radio, smart speakers, and even the computer that runs your car.

A computer is composed of the following basic parts:

1. **An output device** – this is usually the computer screen but it can be anything where you, the user can read information being sent out to you by a computer. The monitor or screen is one example but it can also be the TV screen, your phone's touch screen, and the display on your car's dash among others. Your computer speakers are also considered as an output device.

2. **Input devices** – output devices are the tools that your computer can use to communicate with you, the user. Remember that a computer can't do much except to follow your instructions. So, how do you give instructions to your computer?

That is accomplished through output devices such as your computer keyboard, the buttons on your TV's remote control, your computer's mouse (or laptop's touchpad), your gaming console's controller, and your phone's touch screen among other things.

3. **Storage devices** – your computer needs a place to store information. It needs a space to store the instructions that you have included in the computer programs that you have written. There are different types of storage that your computer can use.

One type is a temporary storage which is your device's memory or better referred to as the RAM, which stands for Random Access Memory. This type of storage will keep on storing data as long as there is power or electricity running through your device. If you switch it off, then all the information and data stored in RAM will be deleted. On top of that the storage space of RAM is usually quite limited to several gigabytes. Other forms of storage are much bigger.

Another more permanent type of storage is found in your hard drives, external storage devices, solid state drives, USB or thumb drives, and CDs or DVDs (yes, there are still some folks who use them). These types of storage devices can store data or information a lot longer than your computer memory can.

That means even if you turn the power off, the data is still stored in a drive. The only times when your data is lost is when you delete the data, erase the whole drive (that means you delete all of the drive's content), or when your hard drive etc. gets broken.

4. **Processor** – this is the most important part of your computer. This part of every computer is called the CPU or the

central processing unit. It's a chip that is embedded in your computer. Yes, it's a computer chip no bigger than your credit card.

This is the brain of your computer. It is designed to take all the information that you feed into it (including the commands that you write in your computer code) and then process it so that your computer can accomplish or perform the commands that you gave it through your program (or through the input devices mentioned earlier).

How Does Your Computer Talk?

A computer is an electronic device and it communicates with other devices that are connected to it. The communication of course is through electronic signals. That is basically how it can send data signals to speakers that are converted to music. Different electronic signals are also sent to your phone's screen so that different colors, shapes, and figures are displayed on it.

The electric signals used by your computer are actually binary – yes, it is in base 2 since a computer can only understand on and off signals (i.e. 0 for off and 1 for on). That means they use sequences of ones and zeroes to represent letters, numbers, and pretty much every kind of data. That means it uses combinations of zeroes and ones to represent data or information.

So, let's say a computer will count from zero to 8 it would do use the following binary combinations:

Decimal	0	1	2	3	4	5	6	7	8
Binary	0	1	10	11	100	101	110	111	1000

Now, don't worry too much about binary coding and binary representation. You won't have to do all of that manually so that you can create computer programming code. You certainly don't need to think about all of that in Java programming because the Java platform has taken care of all that for you.

We're just trying to help you get a grasp of how computers communicate. Now, going back to the binary signals—to organize information further your computer also puts the binary signals into groups of 8 signals—also known as a *byte*.

A byte is composed of 8 bits (aka 8 signals that are either ones or zeroes).

A single character like the letter "a" requires one byte. 1 byte is also the size or unit of computer memory or RAM. Do you remember how your ISP would tell you the speed of your internet into megabytes? Sometimes they tell you that your internet speed is 20 megabytes per second? Well, they usually tell you it is 150 megabits per second to kind of sound so cool, when that actually translates to around 20 megabytes per second—but that is already pretty fast though.

Well, 1 megabyte is actually a million bytes. 20 megabytes per second internet speed means that your internet is able to transmit 20 million characters per second. That's how fast today's internet can be.

So, your computer deals with numbers and all sorts of data using groups of 8 bits (or 1 byte). That was how it was designed decades ago with the old computers. However, as technology has become much better, our modern day computers can work with larger chunks of data. A lot of the computers today can work with 64 bits at a time. In other words modern computers can work with 64 memory allocations at a time.

What Has All of That Got to Do With Java Programming?

Learning all of that will help you grasp a few important programming principles. So here goes—let's say that you want to make a computer compute for the sum of 1 + 1. The first thing you need to do is to think of a few logical steps how to do that.

Think of a computer as an overly simplistic person who can do rapid math (or just rapid anything) but just is totally dependent on someone who will tell them the steps that they need to do.

Here are the steps that you need to do in order to get that addition done (aka the set of instructions so that a computer can add 1 plus 1:

1. Open a memory allocation and call it A and the store the value/number 1 in there.
2. Open another memory allocation and call it B and then store the value/number 1 in there as well.
3. Add the values/numbers stored in A and B and store the results in a third location called C.
4. Display the value/content of memory allocation C

Now, that sounds like a logical set of steps that looks simple enough to follow. Even a child should be able to follow those instructions. A computer of course can do all of those steps really fast.

Introducing the Algorithm

What we have done so far is to create a logical set of steps that will solve the problem that we proposed (i.e. adding 1 + 1). That is actually a programming phase which is called creating or formulating an **algorithm**.

What is an **algorithm**? A common textbook definition of the word is that it is a series of logical steps or a process that is used to solve a problem. As you can see from the steps described earlier, the instructions tackle the problem one step at a time until the process comes up with a solution.

Remember that an algorithm can be as simple as you want it to be or as complex as you want it to be. It's all up to you. You see, there is usually more than one way to solve a problem. That means you can formulate different algorithms to solve the same problem. However, as a rule of thumb, you will want the steps or process of the algorithm to be as efficient as it can be no matter how many steps you include in your solution.

Getting Things Translated

Going back to the initial problem that we introduced earlier (i.e. making a compute radd 1 + 1), now we have a set of instructions (i.e. your algorithm) to solve the problem, the next thing you need to do is to translate that into instructions that a computer can understand.

Remember that a computer doesn't speak English or any other human language. As it was explained earlier, you need to translate all those instructions to a series of binary signals.

But doing all that translation work will take up a lot of your time. Remember that each character is composed of at least 8 bits. After that you need to string them up into actual instructions to access computer memory and then do a math operations etc.—in short it's a huge mess.

No one wants to deal with that.

So, you speak a different language and the computer speaks a different one. Well, how are you going to get both parties to meet halfway? That is where programming languages like Java come in. Think of a programming language as a go-between language that both computers and also human beings can understand—well so to speak, we'll clarify the details behind that in a little bit.

The goal here is to make the computer understand your instructions. There are two phases that will happen before you can accomplish that. The first step is to write your algorithm using a programming language. Yes, a go between language between you and the machine.

Well, computers still can't completely understand all the stuff that you will write even though it is already in Java code. And that is where step 2 comes in (2 steps remember?)—your Java code will then be processed by a program called a compiler.

As it was explained earlier when we covered the components of the Java platform, a compiler is a program or app that translates your programming code into machine readable instructions (aka instructions that your computer can understand).

There are actually a few more things that will happen in the background like a pre-compiling step as well as accessing Java libraries (mentioned earlier), then there is the actual translation into binary codes via an assembler, and more lines of code added to your original code that you wrote.

Again, all of that happens in the background. As a Java programmer you shouldn't worry about that because the Java platform was developed to handle all of that. It's fun to know and maybe when your programming skills have leveled up then you can go into the low level programming details yourself.

Java Virtual Machine

Now there is one last bit of preliminary info that you should know about before we can dive right into writing your Java programming code. And that is the Java Virtual Machine.

There is a recurring problem about the different types of hardware and software that are available in different devices today. The hardware and software components of a smart phone will behave differently compared to that of your car or maybe your laptop.

To make things more complicated, the combination of different processor chips, different operating systems, and different arrays of electrical components will mean different ways to compile (or translate) the code you have written. You need to make machine code specific to the platform of the device that you are programming.

So, what is the Java Virtual Machine or JVM? It is a program or application that is designed to run computer programs on any device or machine. It was quite a revolutionary program when it was released in 1995 and it is still a huge innovation today.

It solved the dilemma that was described earlier. Think of the JVM as a kind of virtual computer inside your computer. It actually has two main functions. The first one is to run any program on any device and on any operating system or software.

This is summarized in the principle of "write once, run anywhere" – you'll hear that a lot and other programming rules of thumb as you gain more experience. The other function is allocating memory space—and it is very good at managing a computer's memory.

The JVM is loaded on a computer's memory (RAM). It is independent, which means it can run on any device that has support for Java—well, almost every device supports Java today. It doesn't produce code for each type of machine, chip, and software combination out there.

That is just impossible. And even if you tried it would make Java way too large a system since you have to accommodate every type of hardware, software, and operating system there is.

So, how does the JVM do it? It produces its own unique code format called bytecode. Take note that unlike other programming languages, when your Java source code is compiled it isn't directly translated or converted into machine readable language—well, again because the goal is not to make a specific type of code that can run on only one computer platform.

The Java bytecode produced by a compiler is a set of instructions that are in machine language. Bytecode will run on any computer that has JVM installed in it. This also means that JVM runs not just Java code and Java programs, it can also run programs written in other programming languages as well—all that is needed is for those programs to be translated (aka compiled) into bytecode.

On top of that, bytecode doesn't need to be customized so that it can be understood by different devices—as long as a device has JVM then it can run bytecode. And that is how Java can run on any device and on any computer.

Now that you have learned about the important geeky stuff, we can now move on to actual coding in Java.

Chapter 2: Writing Your First Java Code

Before you can write and run any Java program on your computer you need to install it on your computer first. To install the Java Runtime Environment or JRE (i.e. the entire Java system with the JVM, the Java libraries, and all the other files), you need to go to the official Oracle corporate website by clicking here.

Instructions on how to download JRE will be provided in those web pages as well. Some of the instructions will include temporarily disabling your firewall and what to expect during the installation process.

Now, your computer might prompt you that you don't have Java (the system that runs Java programs) installed on your computer, then you can download and install it by clicking here. Note: JRE is what you need to write Java programs, but your computer will need to install the actual Java system so that it can run Java programs.

Note that the link provided above is for the installer for Windows operating systems. If you need to install Java for other operating systems like Mac OS X, Linux, and others, you should go here instead.

If for some reason those links don't work or you are taken to a different page, then just Google "JRE download" and then click on the link that has www.oracle.com on it.

Required Tools

For now all you need is a text editor to write your very first Java program code. You can use any text editor that comes with your system (e.g. Notepad if you're using Windows). You can also use Notepad++ if you want something that has more programming support.

IDE

However, if you want to develop applications, test your programming code, and have tools that will make programming in Java a lot easier, then you will need a program called an IDE, which stands for integrated development environment. And IDE is an app that comes with pretty much all the facilities and tools that a programmer needs.

IDE Features

An IDE usually comes with features like autocomplete and text highlighting. It can also be used in the building of executable files. Your Java code is usually saved as a .java file. A compiler will then process that file and return a .class file, which is a file that you can run to test how your Java code works.

Debugging is another important feature of IDEs. Debugging refers to location and removal of programming errors on your Java source code. No one expects you to be perfect but programming errors will prevent your code from running. IDEs have debugging tools to help you spot the errors quickly so that you can edit them ASAP.

Best IDEs for Java Programming

There are numerous IDEs that you can use for Java programming. We can't hope to name them all so we'll just go over the top 3 IDEs.

1. NetBeans

NetBeans was first released back in 1997 and it can run on different operating systems like Windows, Solaris, Mac OS, and Linux. NetBeans is actually the official IDE for Java 8.

Just like Java, NetBeans is open source – that means it is free to download and use. It features semantic and syntactic highlighting. It also allows you to refactor your source code (i.e. rewriting code making it more efficient without actually causing any programming problems). Refactoring is done either to improve the performance of a program or to update it to the latest standards. In other words you are giving an old program an upgrade or update.

2. IntelliJ IDEA

IntelliJ IDEA was first released back in January of 2001. It runs on Windows, Mac OS, and Linux. This IDE comes in 2 different editions. The first one is the proprietary aka the commercial version (i.e. the one you have to pay for) and the other one is the Apache 2 Licensed edition.

This is the IDE for really serious programmers—we suggest that you use this integrated development environment after you have gained a lot of experience programming in Java. You can call this the deep dive IDE.

Two of the unique and powerful features of IntelliJ IDEA include flow analysis and cross language refactoring. It also provides support for other JVM based languages—yes there are other programming languages that also use JVM.

3. Eclipse

Eclipse is another advanced integrated development environment. In fact, this one is solely dedicated and specialized for the development of Java programs. Well, it also supports other programming languages as well, which makes it a very powerful tool. In case you have reached the point of being able to combine different programs written in different programming languages then you might want to consider getting this IDE.

If you are a beginner then that will be some time in the future. Now, there are two versions of Eclipse. There is a cloud version of this IDE which is called Eclipse Che and there is the good old desktop version, which you can download on your computer.

Both of these versions come with an entire suite of tools, apps, and plugins that make programming work a whole lot easier. It even comes with its own custom compiler. This IDE is loaded with a lot of useful features. For instance, if you want to focus on developing plugins for programs that have already been written, Eclipse has a Plugin Development Environment. It has all the tools you need to create and improve plugins.

There are a lot of other IDEs of course. You can find them by just Googling "best Java IDEs". There are free IDEs and there are commercial ones as well. You can try the three mentioned here or you can investigate other IDEs out there. The choice is yours.

Here's a short list of IDEs that you can find out there:

- JDeveloper
- Greenfoot
- DrJava
- Codenavy
- Xcode
- MyEclipse
- BlueJ

The "Hello World!" Program

Now this next part is a bit of tradition. A lot of programmers start with this little bit of code to help them get started with learning how write source code no matter what programming language you are trying to learn.

Following that tradition (sort of) we will begin with displaying some simple text on the screen using the Java programming language. And that text is "Hello World!" Open your text editor – it can be just Notepad or Notepad++ or whatever text editor you want to use.

If you downloaded an IDE you can launch that too. After that, type the following lines of code:

```
public class HelloWorldProgram {
    //This program will display a message on screen
    public static void main(String[] args)
    {
        System.out.println("Hello World!");
    }
}
```

When the Java code above is compiled and executed/run it will display the line "Hello World!" on the screen. This is already a complete Java program albeit a simple one. Let's go over some of the important points about this program so that you can understand the fundamentals of Java programming.

1. **Name of the program** – the name of this program is "HelloWorldProgram" (see line 1 above). This is a user defined name, which means you get to select/compose the name of the program you're writing.

2. **Class** – notice that word that comes before the name of this program. It tells us that the program that you have written is inside a "class." We'll go over what classes are in Java later. Just remember that every line of source code that you write in this programming language should be part of a class.

3. **Public** – the first word in line 1 above says "public." It describes the type of "class" your program is. This time it is a "public" class, which means all other classes in this program can access the class named HelloWorldProgram.

4. **Comments** – line 2 in the program above begins with "//". That means that it is a comment. Comments are part of the source code that are not compiled and converted to machine

code. They are placed there to describe to you, the human user, what certain parts of the source code is for.

5. **Method** – Line 3 has the following: "public static void main(String[] args)". This is called a method in Java programming. It begins with that line and it includes all the other lines within the pair of curly brackets that follow "{ }".

A method in Java programming is any block or group of code that is executed or run after the name of that block is called. That also means our entire HelloWorldProgram is also technically a method.

Here are the parts of the method we just declared in this program:

Chapter 3: Basic Language Constructs

In this chapter we will expand on the things that you have learned when you wrote your very first Java source code.

Keywords and Identifiers

Just like any human language, Java also has its own special words—they're called **keywords**. These words already mean something in this programming language. On the other hand, there are programming elements that you, the user/programmer, can create or compose like the name of the program such as HelloWorldProgram—they are called *identifiers*.

Programming Tip: you can't use keywords as identifiers. If you do that the compiler will return an error.

Here is a list of keywords in Java:

- abstract
- assert
- boolean
- break
- byte
- case
- catch
- char

- class
- continue
- default
- do
- double
- else
- enum
- extends
- final
- finally
- float
- for
- if
- implements
- import
- instanceof
- int
- interface
- long
- native
- new
- null
- package
- private
- protected
- public
- return
- short
- static
- strictfp
- super

- synchronized
- switch
- this
- throw
- throws
- transient
- try
- void
- volatile
- while
- const (reserved but is currently no longer used)
- goto (reserved but is currently no longer used)
- true (reserved word but is actually a literal)
- false (reserved word but is actually a literal)
- null (reserved word but is actually a literal)

Remember that you can't use these keywords and reserved words as names of programming constructs.

Tips for Identifier Use

The Java programming language allows you to create *identifiers* such as names of programs and others. Identifiers are programming constructs that can be user defined or predefined and reserved (aka it is a keyword). User defined identifiers help you customize the programming code. In Java you can provide user identified identifier names of labels, variables, methods, and classes.

Consider the following example:

```java
1  public class Test
2  {
3      public static void main(String[] args)
4      {
5          int a = 20;
6      }
7  }
```

In this example there are 5 identifiers:

1. *a* – this is a name of a variable that is user defined

2. **args** – this is another variable name that is also user defined

3. **String** – this is a system reserved identifier

4. **main** – this is the name of the method, i.e. a user defined identifier

5. **Test** – this is the name of a class, which is also user defined.

Rules for Naming User Defined Identifiers

The rules for identifier names in Java are pretty much the same with other programming languages such as C++, C, C# and others. Of course there may be a few differences as well.

Here are the rules that you must remember:

1. You can't use the reserved words mentioned above.
2. There is no limit to the number of characters that you can use as the identifier name. However, it is not efficient to make names really long. Best practice dictates that you should use 4 to 15 characters only, which should make your source code descriptive enough to make it easy to trace and understand manually.

3. The names of the identifiers you use in Java are case sensitive. That means "mYprogram" is different from "MyProgram."
4. Remember that the identifier names that you use should not start with a number (i.e. digits from 0 to 9). For example, 007JamesBond is not acceptable and will return an error.
5. The only allowed characters to be used as user defined identifiers are characters, numbers (0 to 9), dollar sign ($), and an underscore "_" – so for instance: You_Geek$100 is valid while You@Geek is not allowed.

Different Types of Comments

As it was mentioned earlier, comments aren't executed or even compiled in Java (or in any other programming language for that matter). They provide info and they are used to explain the different parts of the source code.

Programming Tip: At times you can also use them to hide chunks of source code.

You do that to find which part of your source code is causing all the trouble. You temporarily make the working parts a comment so you can isolate the parts that you suspect are causing an issue.

So, what are the different types of comments in Java?

1. *Single Line Comments*

You've seen single line comments in the examples we have shown so far—it's the ones with the "//". You use them if you only want to make a comment on one line.

2. Multiple Line Comments

Multi line comments are the ones that span across several lines of code, like this one:

```
public class Test
{
   /*
   This
   is
   multi line
   comment
   */
      public static void main(String[] args)
      {
         int a = 20;
      }
}
```

As you can see from the example above, the lines of comments start with "/*" and it ends with "*/".

3. Documentation Comment

The documentation comment is for making documentation APIs, which will also require you to use the javadoc tool. So, for example you created a method (lines of code) that does calculations (aka it's a calculator).

And you called it the calculator class. You use the documentation comment not just to explain to programmers what the method is for but also create HTML files that document what you have done.

So for instance you wrote the following method in Java and then added a documentation comment like this:

```
public static int sub(int a, int b){return a-b;}
\** The sub() method returns subtraction of given numbers.*\
public static int add(int a, int b){return a+b;}
\** The add() method returns addition of given numbers.*\
public class Calculator {
\** The Calculator class provides methods to get addition and subtraction of given 2 numbers.*\
```

As you can see the documentation comment begins with "/**" and it ends with "*/". If you compile your source code that contains that documentation comment in it using the javadoc too, then what happens is that HTML files will be created along with the executable Java program.

If you use that to design a web page or website then other programmers who are part of your team who has access to your directory can see the documentation HTML files and open it with their browser. They can then read the explanations that you have documented without having to edit your source code directly.

Variables in Java Programming

We have already mentioned variables in passing earlier in this book. You may recall what variables in algebra and they're almost the same thing in programming. Variables contain that can be changed or manipulated.

In programming terms, a variable is a part of a computer's or a device's memory (i.e. RAM). You assign a name to that variable and you store data into it. After that you can manipulate the values it contains.

Here are the different types of variables in Java. They are actually called primitive data types. You'll understand why a little later on.

- ***int*** – this type of variable is for integers (i.e. whole numbers that don't have a fractional or decimal part) like 1, 5, 4, and 100 etc.
- ***float*** – this is the data type that has a fraction part like -2.7, 3.1416, and 1.618.
- ***char*** – variable of this type only contain single characters and are always inside single quotes like 'b' or 'x' for instance.
- ***String*** – strings are variables that contain more than one character and they are in double quotes instead like "Hello!", "world", and "Oh no, zombies!" among others.
- ***Boolean*** – Boolean variables can only contain either of two values: true or false. You use them for testing different conditions.

How to Add Variables to Your Java Program

This is how you can add variables to your Java source code. It follows the syntax below:

$$\text{type variable = value;}$$

This is called a variable declaration. It has the following parts:

- ***type*** – this stands for variable type. Please refer to the variable types mentioned earlier.
- ***Variable*** – this is the name of the variable (i.e. a user defined identifier)
- ***Equal sign*** – the equal sign is the assignment operator. In effect you are assigning the value that is found on the right side of the equal sign to the variable that has been identified on the left side of the equal sign.

- ***value*** – this is the amount or value that you want to assign to the variable that is being declared in this statement.

Here is an example of a string variable declaration:

```
1  String name = "John";
2  System.out.println(name);
```

Programming tip: note that every argument like the example above ends in a semicolon ";". Every time you are giving a command it would be prudent to end it with a semicolon unless the syntax will tell you otherwise.

In this example, we have a variable declaration for an int type variable:

```
1  int myNum = 15;
2  System.out.println(myNum);
```

In this next example, you declare a variable first and then assign its value later. You are using two lines – one to declare the value and the other to assign the value:

```
1  int myNum;
2  myNum = 15;
3  System.out.println(myNum);
```

Operators

Just like in math (or algebra or whatever part of math you can think of), operators are used to change the values contained in variables. Just a little review, in the expression:

$$1 + 2$$

The numbers 1 and 2 are the operands and the plus sign "+" is the operator. But in that example we are dealing with constant or fixed values not variables. The same is true with the following when you use variables in Java:

$$Score1 + Score2$$

In this example Score1 and Score2 are operands and the plus sign is the operator that changes the values. Now, in Java there are several types of operators. They are the following:

- Math operators
- Assignment operators
- Comparison operators
- Logical operators

Math Operators

These are used to carry out arithmetic operations. They include the following:

+	Addition Operator	Adds two numbers/values
-	Subtraction Operator	Subtracts the value of one variable from the other
*	Multiplication Operator	Multiplies the values of two variables
/	Division Operator	Divides the value of one variable by another without leaving any remainder or fractional part
	Modulus Operator	Divides the value of one variable by

%			another value but this one returns a remainder or a fractional part
++		Increment Operator	Increases the value of a variable by 1 (you place this operator before the variable e.g. ++Sum)
--		Decrement Operator	Works like the increment operator except that it reduces the value instead of increasing it.

Assignment Operator

You are already familiar with one of the assignment operators in Java – the "=" assignment operator. There are others. And as you should know by now these operators are used to assign values to variables.

Here are the assignment operators that you can use in Java:

=	Assignment operator	c = x + y will assign value of x + y into c
+=	Add and then assign	x += y is equivalent to x = x + y
-=	Subtract and then assign	x -= y is equivalent to x = x – y

Operator	Description	Example
*=	Multiply and assign	x *= y is the same as x = x * y
/=	Divide and then assign	x /= y is the same as x = x / y
%=	Modulus AND assignment operator. This operator computes the modulus of two variables and assigns it	X %= Y is the same as X = X % Y
<<=	Assignment operator + Left shift AND	X <<= 2 is same as X = X << 2
>>=	Assignment operator + Right shift AND	X >>= 2 is the same as X = X >> 2
&=	Assignment operator + Bitwise AND	X &= 2 is the same as X = X & 2
^=	Assignment operator and bitwise exclusive OR	A ^= 2 is just like A = A ^ 2
|=	Assignment operator + bitwise	A|= 2 is just like A = A | 2

	inclusive OR	

Programming Exercise

1. Write the following program.

```
1  public class TestCompOperators {
2      public static void main(String[] args) {
3          int x = 5;
4          x ^= 3;
5          System.out.println(x);
6      }
7  }
8
```

2. Run it.
3. Change the assignment operators that were used in it. It currently has the ^= operator. Change it to the other assignment operators described in this chapter, compile and run it, and see the output. Change the values as needed.

Relational or Comparison Operators

These operators are used to compare the values of different variables.

==	Equal to	Checks if the value of operands being compared are equal	Assuming a = 5 and b = 10 a == b (false)
!=	Not equal to	Checks if the value of operands being	Assuming a = 5 and b = 10 a != b (true)

35

		compared are not equal	
>	Greater than	Checks if the value of one operand is greater than the other	Assuming a = 5 and b = 10 a > b (false)
<	Less than	Checks if the value of one operand is less than the other	Assuming a = 5 and b = 10 a < b (true)
>=	Greater than or equal to	Checks if the value of one operand is either greater than or equal to the other	Assuming a = 5 and b = 10 a >= b (false)
<=	Less than or equal to	Checks if the value of one operand is less than or equal to the other	Assuming a = 5 and b = 10 a <= b (true)

Logical operators

Logical operators can be used to determine if conditions are either true or false. They assume Boolean values. Assuming that a = true and b = false see the effect of these logical operators to these two variables.

	Logical AND	If both operands have non-zero values then the condition is	a && b (false)
&&			

			true	
||	Logical OR	If any of the operands being compared is non-zero aka it is true then the condition is true	a || b (true)
!	Logical NOT	This is used to reverse the logical state of an operation or operand	!(a && b) (this returns true)

Type Casting

Sometimes you need to assign the value of one variable to another even if both variables are of different type. This may become necessary in case you need to convert from a smaller capacity data type to a larger capacity data type or from a larger capacity data type to a smaller capacity data type.

There are larger size data types and smaller size data types. Here is the hierarchy of data types from smallest to largest size.

1. Byte
2. Short
3. Char
4. Int
5. Long
6. Float
7. Double

Shifting from a smaller to larger size type is called widening casting. On the other hand, converting from larger to smaller size type is called narrowing casting. Here is a sample program that performs type casting.

```java
public class MyClass {
    public static void main(String[] args) {
        int myInt = 9;
        double myDouble = myInt; // Automatic casting: int to double

        System.out.println(myInt);      // Outputs 9
        System.out.println(myDouble);   // Outputs 9.0
    }
}
```

Arrays in Java

Think of an array as a data container that can hold more than one variable of the same type. Think of it as a string of numbers. It makes sense because sometimes it will be more efficient to contain different numbers inside a series of containers so you can easily reference one item in the collection without disturbing the integrity of your code.

Let's say you have a team of 10 players in your basketball team and you want to keep track of their scores in the current ball game. You don't have to create 10 different variables—you can simplify things by just using one array that can contain 10 int values.

That way, if a player scores a point, you just reference the variable and the container number.

Here is how you declare an array in your source code:

dataType[] arrayName;

Here is a sample source code that makes use of an array:

```
1  class ArrayExample {
2     public static void main(String[] args) {
3
4        int[] age = new int[5];
5
6        System.out.println(age[0]);
7        System.out.println(age[1]);
8        System.out.println(age[2]);
9        System.out.println(age[3]);
10       System.out.println(age[4]);
11    }
12 }
```

Chapter 4: Methods in Java

You have encountered methods in chapter 2 of this book. A method in Java as it was explained earlier is a group of statements or a block of code that are executed or run when the method is called within the body of a program.

One of the methods that you have encountered a lot is the println( ) method. This is a predefined method in Java so you don't have to worry about the steps that were taken so that it could send an output to the screen.

The println( ) method is actually composed of several lines of code which displays output to the console. Of course not all methods are predefined and you can create your own methods in this programming language. That is the topic we will cover in this chapter.

How to Create Methods in Java

The following is the syntax (or grammar rules if you will) that you must follow in order to create a user defined method in Java.

Method Syntax

```
public static int methodName(int a, int b) {
    // body
}
```

This syntax for declaring a method has the following parts:

- ***public static*** – this is the modifier of the method
- ***int*** – this is the return type
- ***methodName*** – this is the user defined name of the method being created (i.e. you get to create your own method name).
- ***int a*** and ***int b*** – these are the parameters of the method—or parameter list

All of the parts described or mentioned above are part of the method header. Notice that after the method header is a pair of { } and inside that pair is the body of the method. Inside the method body will be a group of statements that will be executed or run.

The following is an example of a user defined method. It has an if–else loop and it has two parameters. It returns the minimum values between two numbers.

```
1  public static int minFunction(int n1, int n2) {
2      int min;
3      if (n1 > n2)
4          min = n2;
5      else
6          min = n1;
7
8      return min;
9  }
```

How to Use Methods in Java

Before you can use a method in your Java source code you must first declare it just like in the example above and you should also call it afterwards in the body of your program. Note that you can also call methods in other parts of your source code other than the body of your program code.

There are two ways to call a method in Java:

1. Calling a method where it returns a value
2. Calling a method with void returns (i.e. it doesn't return any value).

Note that when your program is compiled and run, the statements (i.e. the commands that your computer needs to perform) are executed line by line from the top to the bottom.

Whenever a program encounters a method call, the execution of the lines stop at the line where the method is called. After that the header of the method is processed and the parameters of the method are used. All the statements in the body of the method are performed.

After all the statements in the method are execute either the method returns a value that the program will use or not (the method returns a void value aka it returns nothing). The next step is for the program to continue executing where it left off.

There are two ways to end a method call and return to the main body of the program:

- The end or final statement inside the method has been reached
- A return statement is executed within the body of the method.

The following is an example of a Java program that creates a method and calls it as well.

```
public class ExampleMinNumber {

    public static void main(String[] args) {
        int a = 11;
        int b = 6;
        int c = minFunction(a, b);
        System.out.println("Minimum Value = " + c);
    }

    /** returns the minimum of two numbers */
    public static int minFunction(int n1, int n2) {
        int min;
        if (n1 > n2)
            min = n2;
        else
            min = n1;

        return min;
    }
}
```

Methods That Don't Return a Value

As stated earlier, you can also create methods that do not return a value. You accomplish that by using the void keyword. Just remember that the call to a void method is done via a statement (i.e. it is a line that has a semicolon at the end).

```
public class ExampleVoid {

    public static void main(String[] args) {
        methodRankPoints(255.7);
    }

    public static void methodRankPoints(double points) {
        if (points >= 202.5) {
            System.out.println("Rank:A1");
        }else if (points >= 122.4) {
            System.out.println("Rank:A2");
        }else {
            System.out.println("Rank:A3");
        }
    }
}
```

Chapter 5: Java Statements

What is a statement in Java programming? Think of a statement as a complete sentence in English. Simply put, a statement in Java is a command that is a complete command and it can be understood by the compiler. It should contain all the essential details including the semicolon at the end.

There are three types of statements in Java:

1. **Declaration Statements** – these are statements that we use to declare variables.
2. **Expression Statements** – these statements can create objects, call methods, and change the value of variables.
3. **Control Flow Statements** – these statements change the order in which statements are executed, such as looping for instance.

Here are examples of the three types of statements in Java:

```java
//declaration statement
int number;
//expression statement
number = 4;
//control flow statement
if (number < 10 )
{
   //expression statement
   System.out.println(number + " is less than ten");
}
```

45

Output Statements in Java

There are actually three statements that you can use to send output to the screen. You have already seen one of them in the examples that we have provided. The three output statements are:

- System.out.println( )
- System.out.print( )
- System.out.printf( )

Note that the standard output is the screen of the device. You can also output to a file in Java but that would be for later.

In these statements "System" is a class and then "out" is a field which is public and static as well. Its role is to accept output data. We'll go over these terms later in object oriented programming.

Remember: the println( ) statement will display the string inside the double quotes.

Difference between the Three Output Statements

You might be wondering why in the world should there be three different statements that perform the same function. Well, the thing is they don't do the exactly the same thing. Here are the differences between these three output statements.

- print( ) – this one prints strings that are inside quotes and will only print in the same line on the screen.
- println( ) – this one also prints strings to the screen but after doing so will move the cursor to the beginning of the next line below the current

line. It's like typing a line of text and then hitting "enter" on your keyboard.
- printf( ) – this output statement also prints to the screen but it gives you some formatting options.

The following is a program that demonstrates the difference between the print( ) and the println( ) statements:

```
1  class Output {
2      public static void main(String[] args) {
3
4          System.out.println("1. println ");
5          System.out.println("2. println ");
6
7          System.out.print("1. print ");
8          System.out.print("2. print");
9      }
10 }
```

Programming Tip: In case you want to output the value contained in variables, don't put them in quotation marks. Here's an example:

```
1  class Variables {
2      public static void main(String[] args) {
3
4          Double number = -10.6;
5
6          System.out.println(5);
7          System.out.println(number);
8      }
9  }
```

Programming Tip: you can join strings and other data together (also called concatenation) when you want to output them to the screen. You will use the "+" operator to join them together before sending them out for output.

Here's an example on how you can do that with strings and also with variables:

```
1  class PrintVariables {
2      public static void main(String[] args) {
3
4          Double number = -10.6;
5
6          System.out.println("I am " + "awesome."
7          System.out.println("Number = " + number
8      }
9  }
```

The printf( ) Statement

The printf( ) statement is slightly tricky but it is very useful in case you want to make your screen output look more organized. It has the following syntax:

System.out.printf("format-string" [, arg1, arg2, ...]);

The "format-string" part can contain format specifiers as well as literals. The arg1, arg2, etc. part are of course the arguments to be used in formatting the output. They will only be needed if there are format specifiers indicated in the "format-string" part.

Format specifiers should appear according to the following sequence:

1. %
2. [flags]
3. [width]
4. [.precision]
5. conversion character

Note that the items in that list that have square brackets are optional but if these parameters are included they take precedence over conversion characters.

Flags

Flags setup certain page formatting for the output to the screen. They include the following:

-	Left justifies the text. Note that the default is for text and numbers to be right justified
+	Outputs either a plus or minus sign if you're outputting numerical values
0	A zero flag will force numeric output to be zero padded.
,	This is a grouping separator to be used for numbers that are greater than 1,000
Space	This is used for numbers. A space will produce a negative sign for negative numbers and a space for positive numbers

Width

This is short for field width. This will determine the minimum number of characters that will be used for displaying the output. Note that spaces, commas, decimal points, and other punctuations will be included in the character count. Numbers will also be rounded off according to the specified width.

Precision

This specifier restricts the output according to the conversion that was performed. This will limit the number of digits that will be displayed for fractional numbers or floating point numbers. It also limits the length of a substring that will be extracted from a string variable. This also rounds off numbers to a specified precision.

Conversion Characters

The following are your options for conversion characters:

n	This stands for a new line – best practice is to use %n so that your source code can work with all operating systems and platforms
h	Hashcode – this works like an address and is used for printing references.
s	String – note that if you use capital S then all characters will be in capital letters
c	Stands for character – note that if you use capital C then the output will be in capital letters
f	Floating point numbers (double, float)
d	Stands for decimal integers (i.e. long, int, short, byte)

Assigning String Class format( )

In Java you can also create your string format first and then assign it to a variable. That way you don't have to write the entire format you want over and over again in your source code.

To do that you will have to use the **format( )** method. Here is a sample statement that demonstrates its syntax:

```
1    String grandTotal = String.format("Grand Total: %,.2f", dblTotal);
```

Input Statements in Java

To get input in Java you need to use the Scanner object. We will explain what objects are in this programming language in the next chapter. In order for you to use this object you need to add the following line at the beginning of your source code:

    import java.util.Scanner;

After adding that line you can write your source code as usual just like how you see them in our programming samples. However, in order for you to use the Scanner object. Here are a couple of lines to show you how you can do just that:

```
1  Scanner input = new Scanner(System.in);
2  int number = input.nextInt();
```

In the example above, line 1 creates the Scanner object called "input." Line 2 on the other hand creates an input request on the screen where "number" is an int type variable and you are requesting an "input" from the user.

Here is a complete Java program that asks for an integer type data input from the user.

```
1   import java.util.Scanner;
2   class Input {
3       public static void main(String[] args) {
4
5           Scanner input = new Scanner(System.in);
6
7           System.out.print("Enter an integer: ");
8           int number = input.nextInt();
9           System.out.println("You entered " + number);
10      }
11  }
```

Note: you use nextInt( ) which is found on line 8 to request for integer type input from the user. That method is only for integer type inputs. You will use different input methods for other data types, check out the following:

Long	nextLong( )
Float	nextFloat( )
Double	nextDouble( )
String	next( )

The following is a sample Java program that makes use of these different input methods.

```java
import java.util.Scanner;
class Input {
    public static void main(String[] args) {

        Scanner input = new Scanner(System.in);

        // Getting float input
        System.out.print("Enter float: ");
        float myFloat = input.nextFloat();
        System.out.println("Float entered = " + myFloat);

        // Getting double input
        System.out.print("Enter double: ");
        double myDouble = input.nextDouble();
        System.out.println("Double entered = " + myDouble);

        // Getting String input
        System.out.print("Enter text: ");
        String myString = input.next();
        System.out.println("Text entered = " + myString);
    }
}
```

Control Flow Statements

You have already seen declarations statements and a few expressions. You have also seen statements that call methods. Later you will learn about expressions that can create programming constructed called objects in Java. In this section we will go over the different control flow statements used in this programming language.

Sometimes there are statements in your source code that will have to be skipped depending on certain conditions. An example of that is whether to apply a discount on a sale of product.

Let's say you want to give discounts only to a minimum amount of sale. That means you have to check if the amount of the sale is at or below the amount you have set. If the amount of the sale is at or above the amount then you can apply a discount but if it is below then no discount will be applied. That is just one example of how control flow statements can help you design programs.

In chapter we'll go through a few of these control flow statements which include if statements, nested if statements, if-else statements, and if-else-if statements. We will also go over loops and also the Continue and Break statements.

If Statements

An If Statement is a conditional expression. It will first test a condition before a body of statements is executed. It has the following syntax:

if(condition){

Statement(s);

}

Here is an example of a program that contains an if-statement:

```
public class IfStatementExample {

    public static void main(String args[]){
        int num=70;
        if( num < 100 ){
            /* This println statement will only execute,
             * if the above condition is true
             */
            System.out.println("number is less than 100");
        }
    }
}
```

In the example above the If Statement will test the value of the variable num. If the value of that variable is less than 100 then the println statement will be executed.

Nested If Statements

Nested If Statements have If Statements inside an If Statement. This is done to test for further conditions before executing any other statements. Here is the syntax for this type of conditional statement:

```
if(condition_1) {
    Statement1(s);

    if(condition_2) {
        Statement2(s);
    }
}
```

In this short sample syntax, either statement can be executed depending on the conditions that were set in them. It is possible that one, both, or none of the statements will be executed.

Here is an example of a nested If Statement:

```
1   public class NestedIfExample {
2
3       public static void main(String args[]){
4           int num=70;
5        if( num < 100 ){
6               System.out.println("number is less than 100");
7               if(num > 50){
8               System.out.println("number is greater than 50");
9           }
10        }
11      }
12   }
```

If Else Statement

The If Else conditional statement is just like an If Statement except that it has a branching condition. That means if the condition is true then the first statement will be executed but if it is false then the second statement will be executed. Either way, one of the statements within the If Else statement will be executed.

Here is the syntax of an If Else Statement:

if(condition) {

Statement(s);

}

else {

Statement(s);

}

Here is a sample Java program source code that has an If Else statement:

```java
public class IfElseExample {

    public static void main(String args[]){
        int num=120;
        if( num < 50 ){
        System.out.println("num is less than 50");
        }
        else {
        System.out.println("num is greater than or equal 50");
        }
    }
}
```

If Else If Statement

This conditional statement can also be used to test multiple conditions. The difference in this approach is that the conditions are in a ladder form that sort of funnels the testing that is being performed. Note that as soon as one condition in this statement gets executed the rest of the statements in the ladder will be ignored.

Here is the syntax of an If Else If statement:

```java
if(condition_1) {
    /*if condition_1 is true execute this*/
    statement(s);
}
else if(condition_2) {
    /* execute this if condition_1 is not met and
     * condition_2 is met
     */
    statement(s);
}
else if(condition_3) {
    /* execute this if condition_1 & condition_2 are
     * not met and condition_3 is met
     */
    statement(s);
}
.
.
.
else {
    /* if none of the condition is true
     * then these statements gets executed
     */
    statement(s);
}
```

Here is a sample program that uses this conditional statement:

```java
public class IfElseIfExample {

    public static void main(String args[]){
        int num=1234;
        if(num <100 && num>=1) {
            System.out.println("Its a two digit number");
        }
        else if(num <1000 && num>=100) {
            System.out.println("Its a three digit number");
        }
        else if(num <10000 && num>=1000) {
            System.out.println("Its a four digit number");
        }
        else if(num <100000 && num>=10000) {
            System.out.println("Its a five digit number");
        }
        else {
            System.out.println("number is not between 1 & 99999");
        }
    }
}
```

Here is another sample program that also uses conditional statements. This one checks whether a number is odd or even.

```java
import java.util.Scanner;

class CheckEvenOdd
{
   public static void main(String args[])
   {
      int num;
      System.out.println("Enter an Integer number:");

      //The input provided by user is stored in num
      Scanner input = new Scanner(System.in);
      num = input.nextInt();

      /* If number is divisible by 2 then it's an even number
       * else odd number*/
      if ( num % 2 == 0 )
         System.out.println("Entered number is even");
      else
         System.out.println("Entered number is odd");
   }
}
```

Programming Exercise:

In this exercise, I want you to write a Java program source code that checks if a number is positive or negative.

Switch Statement

You can use a Switch Statement in case your If-Else-If Statements are getting too long. Using this statement makes your source code much more readable. Here is the syntax of the Switch Statement.

```
1   switch (variable/expression) {
2   case value1:
3       // statements
4       break;
5   case value2:
6       // statements
7       break;
8       .. .. ...
9       .. .. ...
10  default:
11      // statements
12  }
```

This statement evaluates the expressions and compares the values with each of the available case labels. With every case label that matches the corresponding statements will be executed.

Notice that a break statement is used to stop the operation of the Switch Statement for every case label there is. You should also note that the Switch Statement only works with primitive data types, string classes, enumerated data types, and classes that also wrap primitive data types.

The following is an example of a program with a Switch Statement:

```java
import java.util.Scanner;
class Calculator {
    public static void main(String[] args) {
        char operator;
        Double number1, number2, result;

        Scanner scanner = new Scanner(System.in);
        System.out.print("Enter operator (either +, -, * or /): ");
        operator = scanner.next().charAt(0);
        System.out.print("Enter number1 and number2 respectively: ");
        number1 = scanner.nextDouble();
        number2 = scanner.nextDouble();

        switch (operator) {
          case '+':
            result = number1 + number2;
            System.out.print(number1 + "+" + number2 + " = " + result);
            break;
          case '-':
            result = number1 - number2;
            System.out.print(number1 + "-" + number2 + " = " + result);
            break;
          case '*':
            result = number1 * number2;
            System.out.print(number1 + "*" + number2 + " = " + result);
            break;
          case '/':
            result = number1 / number2;
            System.out.print(number1 + "/" + number2 + " = " + result);
            break;
          default:
            System.out.println("Invalid operator!");
            break;
        }
    }
}
```

Statements for Looping

Loops in any programming language refer to statements or expressions that allow the repetition of certain lines of command. Sometimes you need to repeat the execution of certain statements in order to solve a problem or perform a function.

An example of such a task is when you have to print a long set of numbers in specific formats (let's say from 1 to 1,000). Instead of using multiple lines of code to print all of that, you can repeat executing the statements in a method over and over using a loop. This will make your code shorter and more efficient.

There are three loops that you should know in Java:

- For Loop
- For Each Loop
- While Loop

For Loop

The following is the syntax of the For Loop:

```
for (initialization; testExpression; update)
{
    // codes inside for loop's body
}
```

The For Loop begins with initialization process, and then an expression is tested or evaluated. If the test returns true then the code inside the For Loop's body will then be executed.

Here is an example of a Java program with a For Loop

```
// Program to print a sentence 10 times
class Loop {
    public static void main(String[] args) {

        for (int i = 1; i <= 10; ++i) {
            System.out.println("Line " + i);
        }
    }
}
```

Is it possible to make an infinite loop? The answer is yes. Here is a sample program that has an infinite For Loop.

```java
// Infinite for Loop
class Infinite {
    public static void main(String[] args) {

        int sum = 0;
        for (int i = 1; i <= 10; --i) {
            System.out.println("Hello");
        }
    }
}
```

For Each Loop

The For Each loop is best suited for working with arrays. You think of it as an enhanced type of For Loop. It iterates through each item in an array.

Here is the syntax of the For Each loop:

> for(data_type item : collection) {
>
> ...
>
> }

Observe how the For Each Loop works in this Java program.

```java
class AssignmentOperator {
    public static void main(String[] args) {

        char[] vowels = {'a', 'e', 'i', 'o', 'u'};
        // foreach loop
        for (char item: vowels) {
            System.out.println(item);
        }
    }
}
```

While Loop

The Do While loop is a different approach compared to the For Loop. In this loop the block of expressions is performed as long as the condition returns true. If the condition returns false then the loop is terminated.

Here is the syntax of the While Loop:

```
while (testExpression) {
    // codes inside body of while loop
}
```

The following is a sample Java program that has a While Loop in it:

```
1   // Program to print line 10 times
2   class Loop {
3       public static void main(String[] args) {
4
5           int i = 1;
6
7           while (i <= 10) {
8               System.out.println("Line " + i);
9               ++i;
10          }
11      }
12  }
```

Continue Statement

Let's say that as your program executes you think that you should skip certain statements within a loop since they are no longer necessary. You need to have a statement that can make the flow of the execution jump so that the unnecessary statements will be skipped. You can do that with the help of the continue statement.

Here is its syntax:

continue;

Here is a sample Java program that makes use of a continue statement.

```java
class Test {
    public static void main(String[] args) {

        for (int i = 1; i <= 10; ++i) {
            if (i > 4 && i < 9) {
                continue;
            }
            System.out.println(i);
        }
    }
}
```

Chapter 6: Object Oriented Programming in Java

Java is one of the programming languages that support object oriented programming or OOP. In an earlier chapter we talked about the "primitive" data structures that are used in Java. In this chapter we are taking things up a notch when it comes to data structures when we talk about OOP.

What is Object Oriented Programming in Java?

OOP or object oriented programming is a paradigm in programming that is based on structures called objects. Using objects, programs that you write become more flexible and easier to maintain. In OOP both the methods, discussed in the previous chapter, as well as the data being manipulated and stored are placed into one container called an object.

It's like you're using a variable that can contain more than one type of data and it can contain more values. It's something dynamic that you can change. It's like a page off a record book where you can add more information, remove them, change the information, and change how the pages are organized.

OOP Concepts

To help you understand what OOP is in Java programming, we will go over what an object, class, and constructors are. We will also go over the important features of object oriented programming such as encapsulation, abstraction, polymorphism, and inheritances.

What are Objects?

Think of objects as bundles of data—a more powerful variable as it were. Now, other than bundles of data (remember, variables only hold or contain data) objects in Java also contain the actual instructions that create some sort of behavior—in other words they contain methods.

For emphasis: objects in Java programming have 2 defining characteristics. They have **states** (i.e. the bundle of data) and they have behaviors (i.e. methods). Here's a sample theoretical construction of these concepts.

Let's say we want to sell houses. In order to organize the data about the houses we have on sale we create a Java program that has objects we will call House. This object should contain every bit of information about the houses we are selling. Apart from that, some houses will get sold (account is closed) and some are still open for purchase.

So, when we design the House object it will be something like this:

- **Object name:** House

- **States (the data it will contain):** floor area, color, address, rooms, price
- **Behavior:** open for sale, closed for sale

Note that some buyers may back out of a sale so even if we have closed a house for sale we should be able to open it again in case the deal doesn't get completed. We want the action to come from the object itself so that each house object that we create can stand on its own.

Now if we had to write an object in Java code that had all those details including the behaviors and states mentioned in that description above, then it might look something like this:

```
1   class House {
2       String address;
3       String color;
4       double are;
5       void openDoor() {
6           //Write code here
7       }
8       void closeDoor() {
9           //Write code here
10      }
11      ...
12      ...
13  }
```

Now, if you notice in the example above we are introducing another Java programming structure called a *class*. We'll go over what a class is and other details but we just have to go over a few more details about objects first.

Characteristics of Objects

There are three main characteristics of objects that you should know about, which include the following:

1. Abstraction
2. Encapsulation
3. Message passing

Abstraction simply refers to the process of hiding unnecessary details of an object and only showing the ones that are relevant. **Encapsulation** on the other hand simply means the binding of the states and the methods of an object together.

This binding eventually creates something called a class (we'll cover that in a little bit). Finally, **message passing** refers to the ability of objects to interact with other objects.

What are Classes in Java OOP?

As you can see in the sample code earlier (i.e. line 1) that defined the object called House, it began by declaring something called a Class using this line:

Class House {

So, what is a class in object oriented programming? Think of it as a blueprint that you will use to create objects. The first step to creating an object is to declare or define what needs to be in it and you do that by using classes.

Here's another example of a class in Java:

```java
1   public class Dog {
2       String breed;
3       int age;
4       String color;
5
6       void barking() {
7       }
8
9       void hungry() {
10      }
11
12      void sleeping() {
13      }
14  }
```

In this example the states in this class, which is called Dog, are breed, age, and color, which you can find in lines 2 to 4. And the behavior or methods contained in it include barking, hungry, and sleeping.

As you can see in our examples above, blueprints or *Classes* can also contain variables (i.e. primitive variables). However, do take note that there are three different types of variables that can exist inside a class in Java. They include the following:

1. **Local Variables** – local variables only function within a method. Once all the lines in that method have been executed the local variables in it get discarded. They can't be used elsewhere in your source code or even in your entire program.

2. **Instance Variables** – instance variables are the variables that can be found within a class but are found outside of a method. Note that methods that are inside the class can use instance variables in that class.

3. **Class Variables** – these are variables that are also inside a class and also outside any method within that class. The big difference is that class variables are created using the static keyword.

Remember that you can add as many methods inside a class as you need. You can also have these methods access the other methods within the same class. And when you finally create an object using the class that you have designed or written then that object is called an *instance* of that class.

What are Constructors?

This is another important topic in Java OOP. A constructor in Java is a specialized method that you will use to initialize an object. But what if you forget to write a constructor? If that happens, then the compiler will create a constructor for you.

Every time you create an object it should have a constructor. At least one constructor will be invoked for every object that you create using a class—at least. That means a class or object can have more than one constructor. Note that constructors should have the same name as the class.

Here is an example of a source code that has a constructor in it:

```
1  public class Puppy {
2      public Puppy() {
3      }
4
5      public Puppy(String name) {
6          // This is the constructor
7      }
8  }
```

The constructor in this example is found on line 5.

How to Create an Object in Java

Now we are ready to create an object in Java. Remember that you create an object in using the Classes (i.e. the blueprints) that you have defined in your source code. Write the class first and then create the object after. Well, to be exact, there are three steps in order to create an object in Java.

1. Make a declaration including the name for the type of object that you want to create.
2. Create an instance (i.e. an actual object based on the class that you wrote) using the keyword "new".
3. Use a call to a constructor to initialize the new object that has just been created.

Here is an example of a program that creates an object using the steps mentioned above:

```java
public class Puppy {
    public Puppy(String name) {
        // This constructor has one parameter, name.
        System.out.println("Passed Name is :" + name );
    }

    public static void main(String []args) {
        // Following statement would create an object myPuppy
        Puppy myPuppy = new Puppy( "Fido" );
    }
}
```

Running and compiling that program will print the following output to the screen:

Passed Name is : Fido

Note that when the actual instance of that class (i.e. the object) is created (line 9) it is then initialized by the constructor that was defined on line 4.

Using Methods and Variables within Objects

The methods and variables that can be found inside an instance can be accessed through the objects themselves. Here are the steps to access methods and variables via an object:

1. Create an object by using an object reference and a new constructor. You will use the following syntax:

    "ObjectReference = new Constructor();"

    where *ObjectReference* is the name of the object.

2. Call a variable within the object using the following syntax:

    ObjectReference.variableName;

3. Call a class method using the following syntax:

    ObjectReference.MethodName();

Let's go over a sample program that will help us walk through the said steps:

```java
public class Puppy {
    int puppyAge;

    public Puppy(String name) {
        // This constructor has one parameter, name.
        System.out.println("Name chosen is :" + name );
    }

    public void setAge( int age ) {
        puppyAge = age;
    }

    public int getAge( ) {
        System.out.println("Puppy's age is :" + puppyAge );
        return puppyAge;
    }

    public static void main(String []args) {
        /* Object creation */
        Puppy myPuppy = new Puppy( "tommy" );

        /* Call class method to set puppy's age */
        myPuppy.setAge( 2 );

        /* Call another class method to get puppy's age */
        myPuppy.getAge( );

        /* You can access instance variable as follows as well */
        System.out.println("Variable Value :" + myPuppy.puppyAge );
    }
}
```

The class declaration is as follows: "public class Puppy" which creates the class called Puppy. It has an int class variable called puppyAge (line 2).

It is followed by the constructor on line 4 that prints out to the screen. Note also that this class/object will have 2 behaviors or methods. The first one is called setAge( ) which assigns the age of the puppy. This is the first class method.

Note line 10. The class variable puppyAge will be set to the same or equal value of the parameter for the method setAge. The second class method is called getAge( ), which returns the age of the puppy.

The main program starts at line 18. The new object or instance of the class Puppy is created using this line:

Puppy myPuppy = new Puppy("tommy");

The name of the object is myPuppy and the constructor initializes the name to "tommy".

The value of the class variable puppyAge is then set to 2 using the statement on line 23 that goes:

$$myPuppy.setAge(2);$$

Programming Tip: Remember, to access a method within an object follow this format:

<name of object>.<name of method> (<object parameters>)

You can also access the variables inside an instance using the syntax described above.

Conclusion

I'd like to thank you and congratulate you for transiting my lines from start to finish.

I hope this book was able to help you to understand a lot of the fundamental programming concepts along with the very basics of Java programming.

As you can see, the content that you have gone over mainly focuses on the Core Java concepts and there's actually more to this programming language than what has been presented here.

It is my hope that you have enjoyed learning about how programming languages like Java work and will continue to learn more about Java and other programming languages as well.

I wish you the best of luck!

Manufactured by Amazon.ca
Bolton, ON